The TRUTH
Made Simple

The TRUTH
Made Simple

Mr. B

XULON PRESS

Xulon Press
555 Winderley Pl, Suite 225
Maitland, FL 32751
407.339.4217
www.xulonpress.com

Paperback ISBN-13: 978-1-66288-717-8
eBook ISBN-13: 978-1-66288-718-5

TO MY WIFE, MY CHILDREN, MY FAMILY, MY FRIENDS, MY DETRACTORS, AND ESPECIALLY MY STUDENTS. YOU ALL HAVE, IN YOUR OWN WAYS, TAUGHT ME MOST OF WHAT I HAVE WRITTEN HERE. FOR THAT, I AM ETERNALLY GRATEFUL TO YOU. FOR WITHOUT YOU, I DON'T THINK I SHOULD EVER HAVE TURNED TO JESUS CHRIST AND FOUND GOD'S PROMISE.

THE TRUTH MADE SIMPLE FOR COLLEGE STUDENTS

(and for anyone else who feels a need to know)

There is no organization to this work for the truth is not organized. The truth simply is. Each small truth is like one unique grain of sand or a single star in the heavens. Separate, they seem unimportant, almost inconsequential and, when like grains of sand, they are often irritating when in the shoe or in the eye as we struggle to see and make our way through life. But when collected together, these tiny grains of truth can form the most beautiful of beaches and heavenly vistas that lay like narrow paths between the two vast, competing worlds of darkness we must live in. The truth separates the liquid world of dreams in which we often drift from the uncaring world of rock-hard reality that will eventually bury us. The truth is something in between these two binding spheres that are perhaps barren to the eye, but not to the heart as the truth is something we all long for but cannot yet have. The truth is a promise of what has not yet come. And, like the sweet scent of still unseen roses, the truth beckons us to find its source and dwell in the pleasures of its midst.

It is not necessarily by growing older that we gain the wisdom and honesty to truly see what is a lie and what is not for many of the old remain lost in lives of lies and deceit. The search for the truth may begin at almost any age. It begins with examining the source of the pain and the happiness within ourselves and others.

And, when this search for the truth finally begins, the small grains of truth start to come together, forming that beautiful beach, that star-filled night, that special refuge of deep comfort and solitude where our souls can finally wonder and wander alone in a growing measure of peace and understanding.

When life's desperation and chaos, born from both myth and madness, is finally challenged, the truth becomes a very real place, a comforting refuge, a lens through which we can truly see if the direction of the steps we are taking in our mortal lives is finally in rhythm with our immortal souls.

———◆———

In life, truth does not come first, but last.

———◆———

Although we continue to struggle, man is not meant to change the imperfections in this world into a paradise, but rather the imperfections in this world are designed so that man might change himself and choose to find the perfection in the paradise his soul longs for and will someday have if he does not give up the search.

———◆———

What is taught and learned today rules tomorrow.

———◆———

When freedom becomes more valuable than responsibility, the exercise of freedom becomes irresponsible.

———◆———

The path to the peak of a mountain or to power is always crooked. One cannot reach the summit of either without going crooked.

———◆———

If there is any spiritual value in the exhausting climb to the top of a mountain it is in the soul finally understanding just how necessary the valley is for the mountain to exist. And so it is with everything we leave behind us for mountains cannot exist without valleys.

———◆———

Man lives his life in vain if his soul does not blossom and learn to love. For love is the purpose and goal of life as surely as the flower's bloom and the fruit's ripening is to produce the seed for a new life which grows only when the soul, like the flower, accepts its purpose and finally learns to truly love.

———◆———

In this life, we live off of the living. In the next, we live for the living.

———◆———

The untended garden soon produces only weeds. And so it is with children, neighborhoods, and nations.

———◆———

All men should have equal access not to the pleasures and comforts of life, but rather to the responsibilities of performing the tasks that provide them.

———◆———

Each man should accept paying his dues in life to the best of his abilities for nothing is due him without his own best efforts being given first.

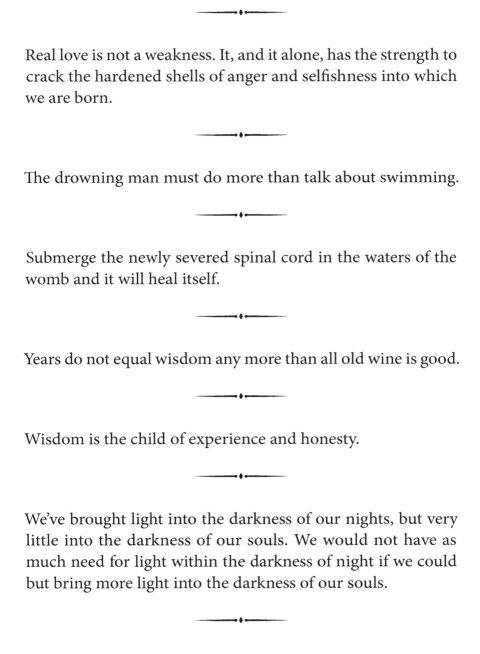

Real love is not a weakness. It, and it alone, has the strength to crack the hardened shells of anger and selfishness into which we are born.

The drowning man must do more than talk about swimming.

Submerge the newly severed spinal cord in the waters of the womb and it will heal itself.

Years do not equal wisdom any more than all old wine is good.

Wisdom is the child of experience and honesty.

We've brought light into the darkness of our nights, but very little into the darkness of our souls. We would not have as much need for light within the darkness of night if we could but bring more light into the darkness of our souls.

A child does not know the truth any more than the child in the womb can see the sun. But to grow, a child needs truth's warmth in love as surely as the child not yet born needs the warmth of the womb.

——————•——————

Truth is like a river of pure water, contaminated only where it touches its banks. There on the banks closest to the truth is where growth is most abundant, but farther away from the banks, the land becomes increasingly empty and barren. And so it is with the soul of man and the soul of nations.

——————•——————

The minds of most men block the truth like rocks in fertile soil, so instead of growing straight, the roots of truth are forced to twist and turn first one way and then another way for the minds of men are most often unyielding. But still the truth is there, no matter how much the rocks have made it twist and turn, and in time, the roots will wear away the rocks, the soil shall become fertile, and we shall be joined to the tree of knowledge.

——————•——————

The person who eats the soup, but does not clean the bowl is still a child and not yet worthy.

The person who complains of rain, but only plays in the sun is still a child and not yet worthy.

The person who complains of hunger, but will not work the soil is still a child and not yet worthy.

The person who expects the truth, but will not give it is still a child and not yet worthy.

The person who cries out in fear, but will not face the danger is still a child and not yet worthy.

The person who thinks his worth is measured by his wealth is still a child and not yet worthy.

The person who is deaf and blind to the needs of the disabled is the most handicapped of all and is still a child and not yet worthy.

———— ◆ ————

The unworthy are like seeds sewn into the soil of life, but refusing to sprout until their selfish conditions are met. And when they do appear to grow, their flowers are without fragrance and they bear only bitter fruit.

———— ◆ ————

The faith that does not respect all of mankind serves man, not God. The man that does not respect all of mankind is not a man in the eyes of God, no matter how much he may be admired by his fellow man.

———— ◆ ————

Understand this, the smallest in life reflects the largest and the largest reflects the smallest. Seek the patterns.

———— ◆ ————

If you know and work your knowledge, you will know abundance. If you know yourself, you will be happy with the abundance. If you do not, you will have misery in your abundance.

---•---

Join the flesh of the cancerous with the flesh of the well and then join the blood of the well to the blood of the ill and the good blood shall heal the cancer.

---•---

That which is and has form does not last. That which is formless and has no flesh endures forever. And so it is with the body and the soul.

---•---

It is common for the young to want to be successful the easiest way possible. But to be successful, they must eventually learn and accept life's fact that the deer rarely goes to the hunter.

---•---

When looking at what we do here, is it any wonder the stars have been placed beyond our reach?

---•---

Everyone wants justice, but is everyone just? Why do we expect from others what we are not prepared to give of ourselves?

---•---

If you wonder about our failings, remember this. Our schools do not teach us to seek goodness, they teach us to seek abundance and greatness. But what is abundance and greatness without goodness?

———— ♦ ————

The force of the hard heart does more damage than the force of the hard hammer. Both can do damage, but one builds only hatred while the other, when used well, can build shelter.

———— ♦ ————

If you are well but not happy, then your life is wrong, for as surely as pain is the unhappiness of the flesh, unhappiness is the pain of the soul.

———— ♦ ————

What does not solve a problem becomes a problem.

———— ♦ ————

One sire, one bitch. One yard, one master. One common milk, one common food. Yet while all the litter's young may resemble one another, they are all different. One is more afraid while one is more bold. One is more affectionate while one is more distant. One is stronger while one is weaker. One is faster while one is slower. One is more curious and one is more indifferent. One is larger, one is smaller. Yet in days to come from each of them will come the very same differences. For from the loins of kings come fools and from the loins of fools come kings.

———— ♦ ————

In life, one does not really see the snowflake, only the snowfall. Learn from this. While each flake is unique, it is when they join together that their beauty becomes memorable. So it is with the truth.

———— ◆ ————

Look at him, look at him, look at him.
　　Would somebody please look at him?
He's so incredibly ordinary
　　That he's really very extraordinary.
Look at him, look at him, look at him.
　　Would somebody please look at him?
Here he is, he's just like me.
　　Take a look and see if you see
Someone so incredibly ordinary
　　That he's really very extraordinary.
Please look at him, look at him, look at him
　　While there is still time to see us.

———— ◆ ————

An idea does not die with the man. It simply waits for another discoverer.

———— ◆ ————

The problems in this world and their solutions can best be shown by asking a simple question: What will/should happen when two hungry strangers discover one potato?

———— ◆ ————

Our dreams tell us who we really are inside our masks of flesh, our new wombs, inside which we all hide waiting to be reborn.

———— ◆ ————

The problem isn't that there is not enough money in the world for the poor. The problem is there is not enough money in the world for the rich.

———◆———

In life, there are always two solutions to a problem. A human solution or an animal solution. What you use is what you are.

———◆———

The life that is yet to come will be as different as this life is to the darkness of the womb from where we came. For as surely as the pain of birth separates flesh from flesh and brings forth life, so too will the pain of death separate the flesh from the body of the spirit and bring forth still another life far more wondrous than that before it.

———◆———

If there is any value in hunger, it is in knowing that what food there is will not be wasted.

———◆———

There are two kinds of hate in life. One is selfish and the other is righteous, yet both cause misery. For what is hated is what is feared. What you fear is what you do not understand and cannot control. What you do not understand and cannot control is called ignorance and weakness. Those who hate either selfishly or righteously are both ignorant and weak.

———◆———

It is your responsibility to learn the value of knowledge and honesty and turn these into wisdom. It is your agony if you do not.

———◆———

Which is truly the more beautiful, that which is beautiful or that which has produced the beauty?

———◆———

Are the more enduring roots and leaves jealous of the flower's beauty that lasts for but a brief time? Which is the more fortunate or the more important?

———◆———

Do not expect beauty every moment of your life, but always work toward it like the seasons work toward spring where beauty has a purpose far beyond its appearance.

———◆———

If cursed with the values of man, how would the unseen wild flower deep in the woods feel with none to admire its beauty?

———◆———

If you would stop to enjoy the flower that will be here for but a moment in your life, then do the same with your brothers and sisters for they, too, are here but for only a moment.

———◆———

Until you start thinking about everyone, you are no one.

Do not dwell on your own beauty, but rather on the real beauty around you. For in appreciating the beauty around, you will become a part of it.

———◆———

It is not what man thinks of you that matters. It is what God thinks of you.

———◆———

To not change yourself is to not change your future.

———◆———

Only a fool tries to fool himself.

———◆———

Do not argue with a rising tide. Let it take its place and then you will see where to build your home. Evil takes its own place. You cannot change it, but you can recognize it and remove yourself safely from it.

———◆———

No matter how beautifully man builds his world, if what man builds cares not for the cold, hungry, and unloved children, it will only be envied or hated. Beauty must have a soul or it is truly ugly.

———◆———

Most people only realize they could do with far less when they have far too much.

———————— ♦ ————————

Watch the earth and it will tell you the truth, and in it, the wise will see themselves. For you are a part of this world, not apart from it. Some flowers bear no fruit while others do. Some young fruit is devoured early and winds arise and sweep away the weakest fruits and branches. Only some survive life's trials, but none survive the final season.

———————— ♦ ————————

While the flesh of the fruit sweetens and withers with age, it also weakens its hold on the branch. The ignorant prize only the flesh, devouring it and discarding the seed, but the wise who see the seed within and what will come of it know the truth. And so it is with the flesh of man on the tree of life. His flesh may be consumed and rot, but it is the seed of his soul, if healthy, that holds the promise of the new life yet to come.

———————— ♦ ————————

You will only truly begin to see life when you begin to search for God, and you will only begin to search for God when you begin to see the emptiness in yourself and the life you live. That emptiness is where God will someday live if you make that choice to let Him in. For in you, there can be God. In God, there is truth. But in man alone, there is only empty blindness. You will understand this when you see your own blindness.

———————— ♦ ————————

There is a God for man cannot create that which does not exist within the laws of the universe. Man can only discover what is possible or already there and he will never discover everything about even the most simple of creations. There is a God, but in this life, we will never know everything about God any more than we will ever know all about even the smallest of minnows. However, that day will come when the God within your soul separates you from the constraints of your flesh and you become one with Him in the greater life yet to come.

————◆————

Why do you listen to the voices of small men saying there is no God when the universe says otherwise?

————◆————

The man who does not have the courage to know himself cannot know God.

————◆————

If there is one purpose in preserving life, it is to give us time to realize that much of what has been taught causes most of man's suffering. Man has been taught it is all right to kill children and both the living and the dead suffer from this lie. Rather than kill children, it is best for those who would not to conceive them. For to live for the pleasure of the flesh at the price of the flesh of the child is unworthy in the eyes of God.

————◆————

We have been given this life so we will come to know the emptiness and misfortune of what it is like to live without God and to have to live so disappointingly with men who pretend to be gods.

———◆———

The beast in the field and the beast in the child are forgiven for they know not good from evil. But the beast in man is not saved, but discarded.

———◆———

Life is the time you have been given to find your way back to God.

———◆———

Harm nothing for sport, pleasure, or faith. Take life only if it preserves life and give thanks for that sacrifice.

———◆———

Respect the oceans and the earth for they are the womb and grave for us, the caretakers who, if wise, will take care.

———◆———

A lie left living holds the truth prisoner.

———◆———

Do not first teach the young to be successful in this world, but rather teach them to be successful with God. When this is done, success will follow as surely as the light of day follows the darkness of night.

———◆———

A rock once set in motion is difficult if not impossible to stop. And so it is with the child who begins to move, right or wrong, on their own in life.

———◆———

If the poor ask God why they have nothing and the rich ask God nothing because they believe they have everything, who is the closest to God?

———◆———

Asking God the reason for an empty stomach is not as good as thanking God for a full one.

———◆———

Neither poverty nor plenty is the path to God for the path is not of the flesh, but of the spirit which should be kept free of the distracting burdens of hunger and corpulence.

———◆———

Man is put here to see who he will serve first, himself or God? The first thing must come first or the last thing cannot last.

———◆———

Evil is like a hungry tiger. It is better to hear it speak and see it prance for then you know where it is and what must be done.

———◆———

If a religion is not for the dignity, equality, prosperity, and redemption of all, it is a prison and not a path for the soul of man.

———◆———

There is no difference between male and female in the eyes of God. Like pillars, each stands separately and they both support a common purpose in serving God who gives life through them. For a man or a religion to believe and act otherwise is for the glory of men and their selfish, blind faith, not the glory of God.

———◆———

God is the truth. He who least serves the truth in mortal life has the least claim to eternal life. And what is one truth? All life is sacred. All life.

———◆———

What wisdom lies behind the silence of animals? And what will they say of you to God?

———◆———

Not the strongest of wishes or commands can break the sparrow's fragile feathery bonds to make it an eagle. We are all what we are. There is a purpose in that if we but look for it, and a happiness in it if we but accept it.

———◆———

When the eagle is born, it still must learn to fly or it is not really an eagle in the fullest sense of what should be. Given this, consider then that when we are born, we need to accept the challenge of learning to love if we are ever to soar off to where those wondrous wings of love will take us. For it is in learning to love that we become, in the fullest sense, what we should become, not merely a man, but a true human being.

———◆———

It matters not what or who you are, for if you have found God, you will become everything you are supposed to be.

———◆———

It is a good person who dies regretting he or she was not a better person who could have made the world a better place.

———◆———

There is no better test of character and wisdom than the use of power and the enduring of poverty for they both demand the best in man or the worst will happen.

———◆———

Sometimes the wisest words are those left unspoken and left to rest behind the warmth of a patient smile.

———◆———

What is in the sparrow that makes something so fragile so durable, so admirable?

———◆———

Those who would argue which religion is true are the least listened to by God.

———◆———

To believe in a religion is one thing, but to believe in God is another for they are not the same. It is the soul that goes to God, not the temple.

———◆———

It is only outside of the temple that you are free to love God and enjoy love and respect for all life which is the true living faith.

———◆———

There is no special hallowed ground for all ground is hallowed and should be treated as such for it all comes from the hand of God.

———◆———

There is no greater misery for a man than to remain a child when grown unless it is the misery and suffering of their own children who follow. To willingly choose to not become a man, a human being, is to disappoint God. Free will is not free. Unless used wisely, free will has a very high price.

———◆———

A man free of God is a prisoner in himself.

———◆———

Men do not carry stones for no reason.

What would this world be like if each of us sought out and held onto the truth like a tree seeks out and holds onto the earth no matter how strong the wind?

Beware of the religion that draws a single path to God for neither five men nor five thousand who believe a wrong will make it right. God did not create you to go to the temple's altar, but to Him, not once a week nor five times a day, but in every moment of every day. For if your faith is not in the heart of your soul, the temple is empty.

Where there is a majority of fools you will find the majority of evil.

What is evil? Evil is that which makes the wise and the innocent unhappy.

The final prophet is not yet born for each person is a testament to God if he but lets his heart say what his soul hears when God speaks.

The young do not yet know the words to life's song, but if you smile and do God's will, they will one day come to listen and learn that music.

———◆———

The word without the deed is a cup offered without water.

———◆———

Children respect most those who frighten, disappoint, and hurt them the least.

———◆———

A child is an empty adult. What society puts in, it gets back; hence, the forgiveness of God.

———◆———

No person or government is wise if they do not think for themselves in a manner that is best for everyone everywhere.

———◆———

Whether it is a man or a nation, the rich will always live in fear if they have poverty as a neighbor.

———◆———

In life, we are both learners and lessons.

———◆———

God waits patiently for every man to wake up. A man is awake not when he sees the truth, but rather when he embraces and follows it. What one does is what one is. If a man does nothing, he is nothing in the eyes of God. If a man does wrong, he is wrong in the eyes of God. If a man does right, he is right in the eyes of God.

———◆———

Heaven has no place for entrepreneurs.

———◆———

Which is better, which is worse? The snake that kills to live, or the man who kills for pleasure?

———◆———

It is a part of the human condition to think bad thoughts. It is inhuman to act upon them.

———◆———

We are ail born animals, but it is through the grace of God that we are given empty souls in the hopes that we choose to fill them with things in life that let us become human beings.

———◆———

To kill the unborn child is to deny the worth of the living.

———◆———

Life with God is real. Life without God is pretend. In happiness and unhappiness, your soul knows this is true even when you pretend not to.

———◆———

That which moves with the tide goes nowhere.

———◆———

To live this life without thinking of others is to not truly live or think.

———◆———

If God gives you a wind, do not complain of how much work it is to raise your sails. If God takes away the wind, do not complain how the oars hurt your hand. For without the sails and oars, you drift not to where you should go, but to where the currents choose. However hard or painful, your fate is in your hands, in your willingness to use what God has given you.

———◆———

The man who works for a living should earn a living. Full labor deserves a full plate.

———◆———

That some receive too much for what they do is as plain as those who receive too little for what they do. To take more than is needed is to take from those who need.

———◆———

To feed and take care of those in need is to feed and take care of your own soul.

———◆———

If the wealthy do not care for the poor, why should God care for the moral poverty of the wealthy? Caring begets caring.

———◆———

There is no joy in poverty, only hope and anger. There is no hope in riches, only joy and fear.

———— ♦ ————

Only the blind can look at the stars and say there is no God.

———— ♦ ————

Life is the chance given to us to see how selfish we begin and how human we can become and to give thanks to God for being given the chance to do so.

———— ♦ ————

Every generation may have different toys and flags, but history shows each generation must face the same age-old tests and problems. For life is a school in which one never knows if they will graduate until the very end.

———— ♦ ————

The hard path eventually becomes easier while the easy path eventually becomes harder.

———— ♦ ————

If you follow the sun, you will return to where you began, but if you follow God, you will return to God and go on forever.

———— ♦ ————

Courage without skill makes for a short contest while skill without courage makes for no contest.

Life is a challenge that measures and tests your courage, your ability, and your humanity.

———— ◆ ————

Ability without effort is like a bird without feathers. It will never fly.

———— ◆ ————

Only when you are willing to examine yourself will you begin to see the truth.

———— ◆ ————

Life is a one-way road. You can't go back. You can stop wherever and for however long you want, or you can go as far as your will and abilities will take you.

———— ◆ ————

Businesses have no interest in the human soul unless they can profit from either buying or selling it.

———— ◆ ————

He who accepts and endures poverty enjoys his weakest efforts.

———— ◆ ————

He who would hurt the child hurts God.

———— ◆ ————

We are all equal in our power to do good or bad.

———◆———

Those who would take life first have the least claim to it.

———◆———

The correct force drives the nail straight. The incorrect force bends and weakens the nail. And so it is with the child.

———◆———

Wisdom is like a diamond. It is worthless if it remains undiscovered and only beautiful if polished.

———◆———

It is no more wise to let a child wander loose in this world than it is to let the lamb befriend the tiger.

———◆———

The truth will change your heart only if you allow it past your ears and eyes and let it enter your soul.

———◆———

The child wishes for life to be good. The adult works to make it good.

———◆———

Maturity occurs when the child that marvels at life recognizes one must work to assure the marvels will continue.

Students like teachers who like themselves. For it is the inner happiness that teaches best.

———◆———

You have not yet lived if you have not yet dreamed of changing the world for the better.

———◆———

A lie only covers the truth. It does not bury it.

———◆———

Where there is no truth there is no man.

———◆———

For your entire life, you, and only you, will be your own constant companion. And only you can choose whether that companion will help you on your journey or burden you down.

———◆———

Once you have learned to walk, blame no one for the direction you take.

———◆———

It is not how many people you walk with in life that matters, it is who your companions are. In friendship, it is quality and not quantity that matters.

The child who gets everything he wants does not get what he needs.

The person who has the least should fear God the least. The person who has done the least for others should fear God the most.

The question should never be why you have no friends, but rather how much of a friend are you?

History has shown there is nothing man can do with his sweat or his steel, his knowledge or his knives, his dreams or his determination, his mercy or his money, his love or his hate that will change in the least the direction of life's drama. For they are nothing more than props in a script that has already been written, carved deep into each generation's flesh.

Often boring, challenging, pleasing, painful, fearsome, exciting, and intriguing, life is a tale whose plot each of us must endure until the final act reveals the Author's surprising ending that reveals how well we played not the roll we were given, but the one we chose.

There is much to be pitied in those who enjoy the pleasures of the flesh and who then can allow the unborn child to die so easily in helpless agony. They are deaf to life's voice. If the infant but had a voice, what would it say? What would it ask? If you listen carefully to its helpless silence, does it not, in the silent agony of its death, already cry out to our souls?

———◆———

If the economics of life has no morality, then it is immorality.

———◆———

If good men keep and protect what they love, even though it may be imperfect, how could a great God do less?

———◆———

Knowledge has no part in your soul any more than the hammer is a part of the carpenter. Knowledge is like a knife that does not care if it cuts a path or cuts a throat. It simply fills your belly, but not your soul and it will not protect you from judgement.

———◆———

The carpenter is known by the house he builds.

———◆———

It is always easier to begin a diet on a full stomach.

———◆———

Your fear of death or lack of it measures your faith in God.

You have read, you have seen, you have heard, you have tasted, and you have touched life, but what do you truly understand?

When a religion or church thinks of its reputation first, it leaves God last.

If you have not yet asked, "Why am I here?" and started seeking the answer, you are not yet truly awake from the child's sleep of the womb and are yet to be reborn.

A man either grows up toward God or he crawls on the earth with the other animals.

For better or for worse, all governments reflect the individual. Therefore, none is perfect and some are most imperfect.

The young of any religion are all victims of man's ignorance. God must come before the faith or there is no value in the faith.

Christ had no faith in temples or in those who maintained them. He had faith in God and was His own temple. Follow Him and build the temple within you.

————◆————

It does not matter how many travel with you. What matters is that you travel in the right direction.

————◆————

What has the most power? That which gives life or that which takes it?

————◆————

Do no harm for your own benefit.

————◆————

History shows man the truth of his own weakness. However, man refuses to open the eyes of his soul to change his direction which is why history is a circular path.

————◆————

The coming of each new generation is a burden. The passing of each old generation is a loss.

————◆————

Life seems to run out of time just when we think we're ready for it.

————◆————

Like a tree, the truth is there whether you notice it or not. But not to see it is to miss its cooling shade in the heat of life.

———— ♦ ————

Where does sacred ground begin or end? Or should it? For all of the earth is one from God's hand and a testament to His love for life.

———— ♦ ————

There are two angers. One is wrong and one is right. The wrong anger argues with what is right and the righteous anger argues with what is wrong.

———— ♦ ————

God does not carry grudges. He measures the heart of your soul not as you may have been, but as you are the moment you come to Him. Therefore, it is best to be prepared for no man knows his appointed time.

———— ♦ ————

To ignore God is to ignore a mountain you must climb to avoid the rising flood that will sweep you away.

———— ♦ ————

God does not expect perfection. He expects you to want and seek it.

———— ♦ ————

Understand this. At any given moment, any government will save itself before it will save you.

————◆————

Never doubt any society's ability to teach its young the skills of painful ignorance and hate.

————◆————

One cannot be good for selfish reasons and be good.

————◆————

Once good, always with God.

————◆————

That which is evil enjoys only itself. That which is loving enjoys others.

————◆————

He who is lost in the darkness and turns away from the light is not only a fool, but truly lost.

————◆————

A man with no money is poor in the eyes of man, but a man with no morals is poor in the eyes of God.

————◆————

He who cannot control himself will not be able to control his child.

———◆———

Disrespect earns its own reward.

———◆———

How much should the elephant worry about trampling on the mouse? And how much should the mouse blame the elephant for trampling on him? Some things in life are unavoidable. Some errors and some pain are simply a part of life and uncorrectable. Learn from this. Except for yourself, very few things, if anything at all in this life, will see you as being important.

———◆———

The longer the life, the greater the distance from God, but also the greater the opportunity to find Him.

———◆———

If a man should see no value in another, then God shall see no value in him for God did not create this life for just one man.

———◆———

When it comes to governments, it is not a question of tyranny yes or tyranny no, but rather of how much.

———◆———

There are times when just asking a question is the answer.

As surely as there are times when the ear needs silence, there are times when the soul must tell the mind to keep quiet.

A mindless soul is a better friend than a soulless mind.

The force of the bow and the aim of the archer are with the arrow all through its flight. And so it is with children.

A good wind never hurt a bad arrow, but a bad wind is never good for any arrow.

You cannot get to where you should go by going to where you shouldn't go unless you change direction.

There will always be those who do not listen to wisdom. They are there for the wise to learn from.

To a thirsty man, the clay cup with water is more precious than the cup of gold filled with diamonds. It is what is needed within that gives value. To satisfy the thirst of your soul, ask what is needed within you and seek it.

———◆———

Strong drink comforts the weak person.

———◆———

As surely as hunger reveals the value of food, so, too, do hard times reveal what is really valuable.

———◆———

To catch more fish than one can use starves the future.

———◆———

A disrespectful child is an understandable disappointment. A disrespectful adult is a disappointment.

———◆———

One who carries too much cannot see the path in front of him.

———◆———

It is the wise traveler who avoids the path where others always stumble.

———◆———

If the student does not respect the teacher, he will not respect the knowledge.

———◆———

Let your last words be, "Thank you."

———◆———

Love is harder to learn than knowledge.

———◆———

To be unhappy with others is understandable. To be unhappy with yourself is a tragedy.

———◆———

Each day as you take life's test, your assignment is to determine that which is true and that which is false.

———◆———

A man who is not his own best friend is his own worst enemy.

———◆———

A child must be willing to give up his toys if he would be with men. A man must be willing to give up this world if he would be with God.

———◆———

The selfish take delight in others' failures while the selfless work for others' success.

———— ◆ ————

Mortal life is a test to see if you will become worthy of immortality.

———— ◆ ————

Every man must be his own savior, but in doing so, he helps save others as surely as a single candle helps remove darkness and as surely as Christ brought light into this world and was Himself saved. It is through His teachings that you also shall be saved.

———— ◆ ————

The loneliness of the wicked is their worst punishment now and forever.

———— ◆ ————

The child who suffers his parents and does good is blessed. The parents who makes their children suffer are cursed.

———— ◆ ————

Happiness often comes from learning how to turn the feces in life into fertilizer. Good can grow from bad. Stumbling teaches the importance of learning to keep your balance.

———— ◆ ————

The greatest fool is he who seeks the companionship of other fools.

———— ♦ ————

A loud voice does not turn what is false into truth.

———— ♦ ————

The wind is to the sail as truth is to the soul. Used properly, it will power your journey.

———— ♦ ————

You are not born so that your flesh may live forever, but rather that the flesh may die and release your soul into forever.

———— ♦ ————

Money is not the root of all evil. The root of all evil is a selfish fear that, rationally or irrationally, perceives a loss of advantage in the struggle for life. Evil comes when that fear is acted upon to gain or regain the advantage at the expense of others.

———— ♦ ————

The castles of the rich have foundations built upon the poverty of others.

———— ♦ ————

Ultimately, nature has no favorites.

———— ♦ ————

Ignorance has never raised a happy child.

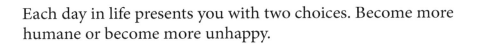

Each day in life presents you with two choices. Become more humane or become more unhappy.

———•◆•———

To not think about what is beyond the stars is not to wonder. Not to wonder is to not fill your cup.

———•◆•———

You will regret growing old if you do not grow up.

———•◆•———

If you use the land well, you will live well.

———•◆•———

He who is given the task of lifting the heaviest weight becomes the strongest.

———•◆•———

THE GIFTS

You have been given an imperfect life so that you might learn to appreciate a perfect life beyond death.

You have been given ignorance so that you might come to appreciate knowledge.

You have been given the pleasure of the flesh so that you can endure the pain of birth that follows.

You have been given children so that you might finally see what you were and understand what they need.

You have been given challenges so that you might understand the extent of your abilities.

You have been given enemies so that you might see the value of friendship and whether you are right or wrong.

You have been given hunger so that you might see the value of labor that brings food.

You have been given loneliness so that you might get to know yourself and appreciate others.

You have been given a body so that you might discover your spirit.

You have been given disappointment so that you might see the value of not giving up.

You have been given the weak so that you might see the value in being strong.

You have been given hate so that you might see the value of love.

You have been given the fearful so that you might see the need for courage.

You have been given the greedy so that you might see the need for sharing.

You have been given abundance and poverty so that you might see the values of opportunity, knowledge, and labor.

You have been given unfairness so that you might yearn and work for justice.

You have been given lies so that you might suffer and come to desire the truth.

You have been given mortal life to see if you are willing to sacrifice it for immortal life.

You have been given everything you need to see if you might truly become a human being.

Don't blow it.

———◆———

Men do not want the truth until they become tired of suffering from the empty joys of ignorance. For each generation is born into ignorance and must painfully work their own way toward the truth that surrounds us like the sweet and tantalizing scent of an unseen rose waiting to be picked and taken into the heart if we but make the effort to find it.

———◆———

A man does wrong just by tolerating it.

———◆———

All of the world's religions are but tiny pieces of a puzzle left unjoined because man's greed for small things and fear of being alone is greater than a whole love for his brothers.

———◆———

The man who says he loves God, but does not love his brothers is a godless man.

———————◆———————

Each society blindly trains its new generations in the ways designed to save the society, not the soul of man. But it is only when men save their souls that the society can be saved.

———————◆———————

To become human, man must find the truth four ways: physically, mentally, socially, and spiritually.

———————◆———————

Why is it man so reviles and hides parts of the body, yet draws the flower so close to his face. While the flower has beauty to the eye and to the nose, the body has beauty to the eye and the touch. Both are there for the beauty of the coming seed.

———————◆———————

Although they will always argue to the contrary, for any government or any system, its people are like any other material, only a natural resource to be used where needed and discarded when unneeded. In any crisis, the unliving system takes priority over the living system no matter how eloquent the explanation.

———————◆———————

In life, it does not matter how many are willing to listen to the truth, it only matters if you are willing to listen.

———————◆———————

The man who is without God is empty of the beauty and strength that makes a man a man.

———◆———

The truth cannot be built into any religion's temple as there is no stone strong enough to bear its weight. For it is only the heart that can carry such a burden.

———◆———

Not the strongest of schemes or dreams will change the flow of life any more than the strongest of oars will change a single current in the ocean's flow. History shows the only choices man has in the boat of life are to drift aimlessly, battle for control of the boat, or to row together through the uncontrollable currents, waves, or calms. In only one of those ways is man the fabled captain of his soul in life's journey.

———◆———

What happens should happen for all things have causes and purposes that can neither be fully understood or denied no matter how great our agony or our wishes for something more comfortable.

———◆———

TO YOUTH, A WORD OF CAUTION

You are such a rare cloth, sewn with dreams
    Soon to be tattered by abrasive age
That will give to you a new cloak of schemes,
    Pressured and yielding to smiles and rage.
What was bad when young will soon be sage
    In life for how it says you must provide
Such meager sustenance for each life's page
    Of tragedy that truth knows is a needless lie.
Take a look at life's rich derelicts.
    Of youth drowned in greed's alluring seas.
Of ignorance where their dreams, now in neglect,
    Lie abandoned like skeletal trees,
Dead and stripped of shading leaves,
    Now unable to hide the lie from its expense
That bends men down on callused knees
    To receive deserter's recompense.

Loved fools, take your chance with dreams
    And leave to others their glittering oceans
That may make your life seem but a narrow stream,
    A dull shadow to their silvered motion.
Pray luck or guilt may prod them circumspect
    Back to their earlier, simpler devotions
Like soothing salves to heal their raped respect
    If they have enough honor left to accept.

Take your time and look at our humankind.
    Then if you will join that poor man's pot
Where excess fat goes to the thinnest mind
    That gorges itself on the slaughtered lot.
Of those drowned and down life drunk sots

Who were unmerciful, but now beg for some
As though the rules of the past must be forgot
    When they are the fallen ones.

Youth, beware the ruling crown of adulthood
    For it has never been worn very well.
Leaving monuments, but also blood not understood
    As the price for the stories they tell
Of dismembered life and putrid smell

That fouls the air and chokes the breath
    While in the distance new flags and bells
Cry out for only a few more deaths.

I know I point a dreary picture,
    But this pain I feel for being so mortal
And unable to spare you this with an elixir
    That God keeps to Himself behind death's portal
Is more than I can stand as agony's expression
    Of disdain is my only defense to startle
Off a whole life's growing depression
    At watching man so bloody, yet artful.

Your mind shall never understand
    What it sees in just one day,
Much less the total span
    Of life revealed in such a clever way
That all manner of things men stupidly obey.
    So, avoid the new mental circumcision
That promises to reveal truth's head in a way
    That requires only a few more bloody incisions.

Life comes but once to each of us,
    So live it honestly with yourself and others
Or life and death shall become analogous.

Opposites the same if you fear your brothers
From same abode, same earth, the mother
On whose gigantic breast we siblings feed
By grace of God, flowers of different colors,
But all from same beginning seed.

What you earn you may justly clasp,
But arm the spirit of your soul

To fight off the lust to grasp
Everything beyond useful dole.
Or to fill yourself from others' empty bowls
And then exult with vainful pride
That you've reached the summit of a tiny knoll
Measured by the bodies of those you've deprived.

For possessing wealth alone is a danger
In the midst of deprivation
Because it turns others to jealous strangers
Who will plant the seeds of your ruination
That will grow quickly toward your culmination
Because of your own excessive needs.
Greed is a parasitic vine of deadly foliation
That kills the host and spreads poisoned seeds.

Trust others not once, but thrice
And plant more than minimum need
For men are subject to honest error's price
Just as they are to nature's deed
That as often against will favor the seed.
But trust, when three times abjured,
It's unlikely will the reverse concede
for betrayal will linger for as long as endured.

The softness of love should not be disdained
　　Nor accepted in its present binding form
Unless an unwinged fledgling you wish to remain.
For it's in love the human is again reborn
　　As often as it's found while those most forlorn
Search for life in other empty quests.

————◆————

Only when you know something can you do something intelligently.

————◆————

We struggle for the truth like a seed, buried deep in the darkness of dirt, struggles toward the life-giving light. And so it is with man where the truth comes not first, but last as we try to struggle free of the darkness of the ignorance into which we are all born and move toward the light of truth we all seek in the hopes it will give meaning to our struggle.

————◆————

The sun does not go to the seed; it beckons with encouraging warmth just as the warmth of truth calls to our soul buried deep within the darkness of our flesh.

————◆————

Responsibility can only come after understanding.

————◆————

What you do with power or poverty is what you are in the eyes of God.

———•———

Life is not here for you to find the whole truth, but rather, like climbing to the top of a mountain, for you to become stronger from your efforts to reach it.

———•———

It is the journey that strengthens and makes wise the traveler, not the rest found at the destination.

———•———

The truth is not in the flesh, but in the soul, just as new life is not in the flesh of the fruit, but deep within the heart of the seed it should protect. Do no harm to your body for it protects the seed of your soul that will become your next life.

———•———

The largest cookie is there for the greediest mind.

———•———

Man does not understand death or he would not give it to himself as punishment or to other creatures as mercy.

———•———

We are one with life like the clouds are one with the wind and the sky.

Nothing asked to be born as it is or where it is. That was Another's decision that we should learn to accept, respect, and trust to bring peace to ourselves and our fellow creatures, as well.

The child who stays a child becomes an unhappy adult.

It is the unhappy man who chooses a full belly rather than a full soul.

What the child holds in the eye and the hand is cradled in the brain.

An education that ignores the soul and fills the brain builds a compass with no needle.

For everything gained, something is sacrificed.

To belong to God is more important than to possess the world.

———◆———

How much you love God is measured by how much you love others.

———◆———

Like all things in life, love is not always guaranteed or always equal.

———◆———

A child with two good parents is more fortunate than a child with one good parent who is more fortunate than a child with no good parents.

———◆———

The society that takes the mother out of the home to feed the child starves the child.

———◆———

That which is not equitably balanced must surely fall whether it is a rock or a nation.

———◆———

The nation that does not listen to the voices of the poor will one day listen to their numbers.

———◆———

Parents should be to their children as a trellis is to the rose if the rose is to ever reach its full potential.

———•———

Until you focus on the needs of children, you are still but a child yourself.

———•———

There is not a child in this world that God has not given to you to care for.

———•———

A Beginning and An End

Black warmth becomes an emerging light
    Followed by a grasping touch still not in sight
While the blackness drowns in colored shadows
    Of shapes and sounds and pretty bows
Too soon slapped away with not another glance
    As other things thrust forward for equal chance
To replace what was a warm black serenity
    Now gone in a race between drought and plenty.
Yearning and straining for long lost satisfaction,
    Possessions are held up for inner reflection,
But soon show a design that is sparkling, yet sour
    Like fragile crystals that can last but hours.
Confused and guilty about even our own beginning,
    We are strangers to ourselves with truth spinning
Away from words that reach both within and out
    To put together a being whose pieces whirl about.
We laugh and weep and look around with starving stares
    That cannot see, but always wonder where
We can rest a moment in our race with time

So our prayers and sweat might let us find
The truth which seems gone and fled
     Leaving us alone with a life left unsaid
That still reminds us but in bitter tones
     That we are more than just our flesh and bones
Soon to be torn apart and cast asunder.
     Have we really lived? We'll always wonder.

———◆———

Who is wiser? He who respects what a man is, or he who
respects who a man is?

———◆———

911

Glass and steel in crystaled abundance
     Forsakes the earth in brilliant redundance
Above man fused with fear to his laden bowl.
     A stranger to his off and on neon soul,
He still starves on history's hard-gained fat
     Like a gorged, but thin greedy rat
Racing around under the silvered sun
     That witnesses the death of one time sons
Perishing in a hellish fire for a purpose that
     Is yet to come before it ever comes back.
Men, fools of a privileged kind,
     Do not think your friend is uncaring time
That will comfort wounds with magic years
     That come and go like your endless tears.
You've decided God is only for after death
     And not for life's rabid breath.

You draw in to command and revile
    Others in a most vigorous, but civilized style
Lest Satan you think you cleverly control
    Will exceed his demanding democratic dole
With God and become too generous on man's behalf
    With machinations beyond simple distaff.
Display your flags to show your might
    With columns of wrong against columns of right
No longer living men, but endless numbers
    Forming a living wall guarding nervous slumbers
Of many too afraid to give up their dreams
    And admit they're only ignorant schemes
So valued for their soft pleasing essentials
    That the living wall becomes inconsequential.
Striving to win in a misguided direction
    That protects a lie and shuns correction.
Do not pause except with ritualized wonder
    When it is your own son crushed down under
The wheels of your own hapless design
    Whose demands now take yours and not just mine
For victory is coming; they say it's almost here,
    A promise hidden in the magic of next year.

———◆———

To truly answer the question as to which person is the most valuable to a society, the smart person or the good person, you must instead ask which one is the greatest danger?

———◆———

Beware those who make their living by selling God.

———◆———

There are no buttons to push in nature. In nature, you must learn to push yourself faster than the tiger can run.

———◆———

No man is what he should be, but to be aware of this is what every man should be.

———◆———

Every society demands participation to its standards, good or bad, or it punishes with poverty and even death.

———◆———

The second greatest mystery in life is why some men try so hard to find God. The first greatest mystery is why some do not.

———◆———

Heaven is not as exclusive as some desire it to be. It is not a reward, but rather another step toward God who desires a closer presence of all who choose to need Him.

———◆———

Many men reject God because man has fashioned a god in his own image and is, therefore, too small to be revered.

———◆———

The hand that does not steal for fear of being caught still steals.

———— ♦ ————

If God is infinite, then so, too, must be His love, His mercy, His forgiveness and His wisdom to recognize the difference between oppressed sinfulness and willful sinfulness.

———— ♦ ————

Your decision to begin searching for God is like lighting a small match. The tiny flame will not last long unless you let it ignite your heart which is the torch of your soul.

———— ♦ ————

Although one can be divided into an infinite number of parts, how can even one part plus the infinite balance of parts equal an infinite One? An infinite number of parts plus another part would be greater than an infinite One, but rationally, nothing is larger than infinity. Therefore, the universe is either not infinite or it is an infinite but indivisible One.

———— ♦ ————

Those who can see the world will see this: gravity is not pull, but push much like the unseen air fuels the flame. The greater the fire and heat, the greater the need for a flow of air. Think about it.

———— ♦ ————

Life is a struggle. Never doubt that and do not waste your time wishing it was not so. Focus on the problem that remains which is whether or not you will make it a fair or unfair struggle.

Which is better, to have lived a life of suffering, or to never have lived at all?

—————◆—————

Remember this: heaven would be empty if it required perfection. Like the cook's cutting away of the bruises on the apple, God saves what He can. Heaven only accepts that which is good in you and rejects the rest. How much of you will go to heaven depends entirely on how much you bruise yourself in this life.

—————◆—————

To The Individual

Whether by plan or omnipotent joke,
    Life will produce a rare breed
Of spirit that refuses the common yoke.
    To no great cause will he concede
While pursuing a bidding inner need
    Unfelt by other men who languish
Toward slaughter like sacrificial steeds
    Carrying flags they ignorantly brandish.

Truth his food and faith his measure,
    Upon himself he nobly relies
And finds independence an unhindered pleasure
    That frees pinioned wings that beat goodbyes
To the herd's now upturned and jealous eyes
    Gazing in contempt at his awkward motions
As he struggles to stay aloft in skies
    Out of bounds to ordinary notions.

Men, like a deep soil of discouragement,
  Wait sterile and jealous beneath him
And prepare unkind, gleeful merriment
  To celebrate the defeat of his radical whim
They called a flowered, but fruitless limb
Until it bears golden harvest to their surprise
  And he returns down to a now jubilant din
  That declares itself fertile for growing such a prize.

————◆————

Life is not meant to be perfect for, if it was, man would have no reason to yearn for the perfection of God and every reason to worship himself for no reason.

————◆————

Forgiveness cures the disease of hate.

————◆————

Only doing gets it done.

————◆————

When a man must wrestle with the truth, he will only win if he loses.

————◆————

Knowledge is much like a bag of nails you use to build a house. How well the house can be built depends upon how many nails you have. Collect all you can for the life you build is the house you must live in, large or small, sturdy or weak, comfortable or uncomfortable, safe or unsafe.

———◆———

To plant but one seed is to foolishly try to deny the bug its due.

———◆———

Fools choose foolish leaders. Cowards endure them.

———◆———

No fish expects to be caught.

———◆———

It is not enough to believe in God. One must do God's work if the belief is to be believed.

———◆———

Only God could give life to something as insignificant and imperfect as man and then love him so much that He gives a promise of heaven, as well.

———◆———

A good parent is the one who most understands God's feelings for man.

———◆———

The only good life there can be is the one in which the individual strives to become a better person. If this does not happen, the life is not good.

———◆———

The man who does not believe in God has not yet awakened and lives in dreams and nightmares.

———◆———

Life's meaning is not in just one person
    No matter the love for husbands or wives
Who are rivers known to gently flow or worsen
    Under whatever fortune uncaringly contrives.
Carried on their one narrow tide,
    Your direction and control is not your own
And life shall have you like a mindless bride
    Just as cold and heat are absorbed by stone.

As with any beginning, there is an ultimate end
    And what lies between is balm or lesion
On life's wayward path where your life will bend
    Toward ignorance or love and reason.
For each is known to have their season.
    But dear youth, stay true and never try
To satisfy the ignorance of man, a treason
    Many serve, but can never justify.

———◆———

Life does not belong to you any more than the air belongs to the bird or the ocean belongs to the fish. Like them, we only move through it, enduring its extremes as best we can until, finally too weary, the currents take us to where we all must go.

———◆———

The man who runs from death travels the shortest distance.

———◆———

Those who think themselves most worthy of heaven should be the most afraid.

———◆———

Only when a man truly realizes there is a God will he truly understand what he is, is not, and should become.

———◆———

Foolish are those who seek signs of God for they remain blind and miss the wondrous signs already all around them.

———◆———

It is not your dreams you should follow, but rather the path to God where all dreams come true.

———◆———

You will hear the voices of false gods around you all of your life, but it is the voice of God within your soul you must listen to.

———◆———

In observing the snail, you may make several choices. You may make fun of its slowness or you may admire its quiet determination and patience. What you choose to think, in words or silence, tells you what kind of person you are. You may look for good in life or you may look for bad in life. Most of what you learn to think you learn from uncaring life. What you should think you will learn from those who listen to God. It is then, in listening to both, that you will choose to become who you will become.

———◆———

There are alternatives, but no substitutes for love, knowledge, and courage. Choose well.

———◆———

Life is not fair. That is a truth. You may use that truth to justify what you do or you may accept it as a challenge to become fair. The choice is yours.

———◆———

TRUTH RULES

Avoid excess in all things held in the hand
Care for the poor and infirm
Labor with pride
Rejoice with thanks
Love and respect all life
Take life only when it preserves life
Recognize and face evil even when afraid
Give thanks

Seek and defend the truth
Seek knowledge
Harm nothing for pleasure, hate, or faith
Defend truth and just causes
Forgive
Have patience
Use all things wisely
Do not hide your love of God
Trust and love God before all other things

———◆———

Do not be afraid to move toward God. Be afraid if you do not.

———◆———

Sacrifice nothing just for pride, but everything for God

———◆———

INTROSPECTION

Man's days are numbered, but always unknown
    As each one passes on in crimson defeat
And are added to a life now grown
    Older and more want to dream sweet
Yearnings for what is left still unsewn
    By man who will be judged on his use of life
By the hand which soon will unflesh each bone
    With sharpened years left untouched like a virgin wife.

Dreams are not as good as when done
    For man's mind lays like a wall of clay
Across their path, a barrier to creativity's run

Whose strength and will he daily weighs
To see if it can still live in this trying way
   Where yesterday's efforts are held up for praise
To others who in fooled admiration say
   Glowing words toward which his ego sways.

And then we are alone with real knowledge
   That peers behind what others saw
To see with withered ego the sacrilege
   Of our pride that once felt soothed, but now is raw,
And delinquent to truth and inner law
   That now extracts its penalty of deep shame
For our own deceptions designed to draw
   Forth absurd praise we absorb like earth does rain.

Once, I could not grasp life's temporary presence
   Like a silvered urn soon out of fashion
And empty of life's measured essence
   That gave it sparkle, but also a lesson
To countless others, but not to me who was exempt
   From mortality that gives to all a certain ration
Except to me as though a value too great to pre-empt.

It's the puzzled mind and coral horizon that beget
   The ugly child of time we obey in discontent
For it pays undue and lingering respect
   To sweat and slavery, but not enjoyment
Which it races by as if in fear it might relent
   Like a tempted priest hasty to avoid a sublime
Respite from the agony men must endure to the extent
   Young dreams lose to a more practical kind.

Now, before I am ready to finally accept

My own mortality, death's unseen finger
Touches my flesh in planned caress most adept
At clawing in scary wrinkles to injure
My immortality with a reality that won't linger
Once born, but laughs and races through life
Like a voracious bird who's an off-key singer
Of many talents when it comes to blood and strife.

It is death that should fashion your marker
That must read you saw life as it really existed
Or you will be seen as nothing more than a simple larker
Of purposeless design in a life where nothing
is trusted
In a world with no reason and where truth is resisted.
Don't die before you die with a belief
In a relativity of law that gives you eyes misted
With glittering progress yet to provide promised relief.

Solutions do not rest just in machines or science
For the problem is imbedded in the flesh of our race
Which learns by tongue or other contrivance
To value pleasure and the use of the mace
Which often leads man to not leaving a trace
Of himself for although he is alive
He does not know how to live or make his place
In this gift with no precedent before he arrived.

———— ◆ ————

There is no one true faith on Earth any more than there is one
true man on Earth for man corrupts everything he touches.
But there is one true Light. Seek and find Him.

———— ◆ ————

Like a river flowing around a stone, this life goes on regardless of our dreams.

———◆———

Love to learn. Learn to love.

———◆———

Justice celebrates when there is truth, but truth knows only sorrow when there is no justice.

———◆———

Societies do not teach thinking. They teach conformity to protect and preserve social and economic stability. This is why schools teach to the belly and not to the soul which is left starving in both men and nations.

———◆———

A full belly is no cure for an empty soul.

———◆———

If you are fortunate, there will come a day when, deep within you, you will come to know this life and yourself and realize your soul knows you do not belong here. For in each of us is an undeniable desire for truth, love, justice, and true knowledge, but our souls know they are not to be found here in this life, but in the next.

———◆———

Time is the ruler with which we measure life's endless motion, but if life is endless, then time is timeless and has no measure.

————◆————

If you struggle against God and win, you lose. If you lose, you win.

————◆————

If a man stands for nothing, he'll fall for anything.

————◆————

FOR THE PLEASURE OF POWER

The crowd is cautious with slitted eyes and angry mutters
 Toward painted angels all gold entangled
In richly draped windows above the common clutter.
 There, brittle faced, these beauties spangled
Gaze from earthly heaven as the rope dangles...
 Near the head of Jamie.

Breathing hard, beauty's lad can barely step
 and shuts the eyes that drew her sighs
Away from discontent that dreamed of love surrept
 On king's bed, empty with its own disguise
That ventured him out to find his own vice...
 Oh, beauty's sad luck in Jamie.

White-lipped soldiers behind steel tradition
 Stand rigid lest they might retreat
Before a coming wrong that hints perdition
 If they make the evil complete
By ignoring the crowd's meek entreat...
 To spare the life of Jamie

Jamie, shut your eyes so this ill-woven cloth
    Over your head no longer weaves bars of a prison
Where in blackness as though a moth
    You seek light's and life's last tiny prism
Soon to part with the schism...
    Of your soul and flesh, young Jamie.

And close your ears with fond memories
    To the rolling drum's growling thoughts
Which have no place in sweet, sad reverie
    That echoes her pleas that brought
You to her bed where you were caught...
    Serving your queen, young Jamie.

For no blame will the mighty take
    When judged with the common person
Whose beauty they did want to make
    Until their honor chance did worsen
Beyond repair of even fabled Merlin...
    Feel the rope, young Jamie.

Pity you did not limp or stutter
    In her eyes to make you equal
With your lesser friends she views as clutter
    For then far different, safer sequel
Would be yours instead of one night regal
    And then the gallows, Jamie.

But Jamie, this is life and this is death
    And no hero comes to whisk you away
To give back to you a full life's breath
    For they all want to live another day
But won't if they step out your way...
    To save your life, youn-SNAP!

———•———

THE LIMITS OF INTELLIGENCE

How much sweeter is the scent of the rose
    So sweet and delicate in the curious nose
When the mind cannot turn this delight into words
    And man's great wisdom is no longer sure
As someone asks how it smells
    And genius must pick a rose to tell.

———•———

TO MAN'S PRINCIPLES

To our principles we ignite an eternal flame
    Then put it out for repair
And over and over it is the same
    Eternal flames for perhaps a year.
Get a clue.

———•———

God does not care so much about who you love or how you love so much as does your love have respect and responsibility? For if you love with respect and responsibility, there is no sin in who or how you love.

———•———

Do something good with "now" and "now" will become a better place for you and others.

———•———

HOW MANY CAN REMEMBER HISTORY'S LESSON IN...?

November 1964 when the night was cold and dark
    With man's shadowy and soulless passions
Draining away his hopes of peace away into stark
    And empty nothings, goading futile compassion
With screams of terror that send helpless truth
    Into an ashen and trembling commiseration
For men still mounting crumbling bastions
    Which promise his own obliteration.

Now a forgotten lesson, the Congo Massacre was
    Real in blood, but it did not change what man does
Today, so it is more than easy to simply say
    Tomorrow, too, will be like all the yesterdays.
But perhaps when a million years are past
    And all the blood and pain's been absorbed by grass
After Mother Earth's cough sends men sprawling
    With pride and steel of no help as yawling
He is consumed in her mighty spasms
    Which finally bury her burden in fiery chasms.

And as fond as we are of monumenting our path,
    What will be left after this terrible wrath?
What can be built as a lasting measure,
    Saying we lived for nothing will be left of us
    or treasure?
It's hard to be forgotten, once and for all
    For what will there be to record our crawl
Across the centuries through which we've been deceived?
    For there will be nothing left that will ever grieve

Over our death after treating life with such triviality
    that we took it from others with such finality.

That day shall come and our squandered history's
    Records will dissolve into more useful dust
To become a mountain's misery
    As it, too, is worn down by abrasive gusts
Like man eroded away by his own lusts.
    In providing for our thoughtless stay,
All we build is that which can rust
    And even that we often do in a most miserable way.
For what God's wisdom provides in a bounty of color
    Our ignorance finds hateful in our own brothers
As it shouts in wicked glee at the gush of blood
    That screams ear to ear in a terrible flood
In the name of causes whose avowed plans
    Are supposed to exist for the benefit of man.
Do you not hear today this echo from our crimson past
    That said it, too, worked for truth's repast,
But only made bones of both dreams and men
    By rewording the same plan and beginning again?

Men cannot piece together tomorrow's dreams
    By borrowing from blood now past
Or by arguing the end justifies the means
    Without making his plans another flimsy mask
Covering only more of what he fled from aghast.
    This is an endless race along a circular path
Where only suffering wins in a macabre task
    That plays games of dodge with bails of wrath.

Eyes and mind of gifted sight
    Men alone create the ugly life

For even pigs we consider of low production
    Won't walk a mile for another's destruction.
Yet some men, with their ingenious ways,
    Have turned this globe into a horror maze
And make their living by planning death
    And give this goal their most fetid breath
For reasons that balance out on either side
    As truth with one does not abide
While wrong possessed they ignore or hide.

At the least, men should know what truth isn't
    After suffering so much wrong,
But still they accept whatever is present
    And continue to sing history's old songs
While screaming and marching loyally along
    To face those who bawl a different verse
And force them to change as they are not as strong
    And the chorus they sang was a sound perverse.
Today is simply the crest of history
    From which we view this eternal mystery
Stretched before us with tomorrow's untold
    Like unfurling sails that are eons old.
So, the days move us on, blind and stubborn
    Dressed in clothes we've always worn.
It's our own blindness that causes us the pain
    And stubborn pride, not the devil's stain
Some men use as a most foul excuse
    For a way of life we let grow obtuse
In ourselves and children who know no better

After drinking from the vessels of culture,
    Home, church, and state brood hens hatching vultures

Which promise better days, but end up giving
　　Little more than chaos as a gift to the living.

In wisdom's name, chaos rules in our vaulted intellect,
　　Trapped and ignorantly demanding unbiased minds
To try again the old ways now newly resurrect
　　and draped in flags and slogans of more modern lines.
And so it's been for thousands of years.
　　We build and rebuild cities and bury our dead
And wonder what happened for this is not what was said.

Misery today is no different from that in the past
　　Nor is grief and sadness which seem to last.
No matter what we use to drape or shroud
　　The new colors and names we create to cloud
The old reasons which still shine through
　　and laugh at the deception we take as new.
For until man opens his soul, life will not change
　　As we are the ones who forge our own chains.

————◆————

You are responsible for what you put into the minds of others.

————◆————

What does a caterpillar get for being a caterpillar except a promise of better things to come. To receive better things, the caterpillar must change, and without that change, that crawling, devouring creature will never fly or sip life's sweet nectar. So it is with man.

————◆————

Competition is a vibrant quality of youth that prizes the glory and excitement of winning. But winning, by its very nature, also produces losers. In childhood games this can be endured for it does have value in building strengths of character for all who play. But in economies this vibrant but immature quality of youthful competition can and does have disastrous consequences that can only be forestalled if the more mature quality of knowledgeable cooperation sets the tone of play.

———— ◆ ————

A BRIEF HISTORY

In the beginning void, all was black and still,
    A quiet silence waiting for the commanding Will
That would create all that was chosen
    And deign with grace to give it motion.
Black and white, dark and light,
    Heaven divided into brothers day and night,
Serenity is now gone, split asunder
    Into a new and brilliant whirling splendor
Moving toward an eternal destination,
    The chosen begin their compilation
Of miniscule beginning rudiments
    And build them into continents
On a round orbed thrones on which to rest
    A glittering home unsurpassed.
Forged by fires and roaring smoke,
    Slowly, slowly, stroke by stroke,
A patient Earth lays a floor
    And ruptures her work more and more
To raise mountain walls of bulging girth
    Above red granite bowels giving birth

To even more trembling fluid flesh
  That cries out in a steamy breath
To the heavens above awed to silence
  Over the spectacle of such disciplined violence.
And so the heavens and Earth and willing time
  Follow an unseen, but determined line
Set down by a Reason they do not question
  As to the goodness of the direction.
The seas soon fill and embrace the shores
  While the building continues even more
With mountains polished down into sand
  Lying in valleys, waiting with an eager land
For nascent life struggling in the oceans
  And still unaware of this promised Goshen
With gifts waiting beyond imagination
  of those still-to-come generations.
Then one day, the beach is home.
  Life trembles there, clutching stone
As waves push it to still higher ground
  Where it waits and stares all around.
Dimly wondering at the retribution
  To be expected for this revolution,
Life now joins the bleak and barren vision
  That blindly beckons as a mission
Over yearning wishes for what is left behind
  Down below that liquid line.
Some do return, but some do stay
  And all live their lives from day to day

Growing strong, but still being consumed
  For all will be gone, but later exhumed
By a restive Earth still not done
  As it builds the home around the Sun.

The Reason doles out the turns to live
    With longer time to some it gives,
Years, perhaps days, minutes to some,
    But all must end so better that than none.
For It is generous in giving all the chance
    To help this life toward the final stance
Still left a mystery to those who would reason
    Why everything has a time and a season
And place on this wondrous earth
    That's become a vast organ of prolific birth.
Slime and grasses, creatures thriving,
    Screaming, hissing, running, dying,
And struggling in awesome copulation
    Before they endure the desolation
That takes them away to bring something else
    More adapted to vast sprawling veldts
Or steep mountains with sceptered peaks
    Where swift birds with hard curved beaks
Glide over the bones of the past and dead,
    History's old skin now shed and fled.
And so life goes on to more complex struggles
    Always persisting despite the troubles
To balance on an incredible scale
    The minnow to the distant galaxy pale
With everything having its own special duty,
    But all combined into a special beauty.
All this moves toward a common destination
    Unmindful of one island's possible ruination
By creatures who pray luck will somehow intervene

    To save them from a fate so obscene.
With pride, they will not go very far,

Not even to the nearest star
　　Placed wisely out of reach of greedy hands
　　　And screaming blaring martial bands
That hear and see nothing but their own sounds
　　　That drowned out Reason now out of bounds.
　　For as far as life is concerned,
　　　It has never really failed to learn
　　Or become so completely blind
　　　As to place its future in just one kind.
Which leaves us with just one conclusion:
　　　A choice between a Reason or empty illusions.

———◆———

The nation or parent that loses the value of truth, and the truth of values, loses its youth and it's destiny.

———◆———

Given the weakness and pains of the flesh, who among you would choose the body as a vehicle of immortality? Does the caterpillar mourn the loss of its once creeping flesh as it unfolds its new wings of freedom? Do not mourn the past for what you once were or could have been but rather build the future into what you can be.

———◆———

There is no stronger man in the world than the man who controls himself.

———◆———

Do not waste your life trying to bring the world of man into focus. Focus on God and you shall see man not only as he is, but as he should be.

————◆————

True learning begins when you stop asking others to answer your questions and you begin expecting yourself to provide answers.

————◆————

What does a bird have? Not much, only the sky above him and earth below him. Can we say as much for ourselves and who then truly has the most freedom?

————◆————

Truth is like a sunrise. You must be awake and put yourself in position to see it.

————◆————

Our lives do not so much reflect reality as they reflect our dreams which is why life so often turns into nightmares.

————◆————

If you do not change yourself, you will not change your future. If you do not change society, society will have no future for society, good or bad, is nothing more than an enlarged reflection of man's collective and developmental nature.

————◆————

The ignorant want to know only the truth they want to believe in.

————◆————

Whether it is lies or truth, we are what we believe. What we believe is what we do. What we do we are accountable for.

————◆————

The world will try to buy and sell your soul if it thinks there is a profit to be made. But is it for sale? That is the eternal question each of us must answer every day we are given.

————◆————

The world tempts all and fools all except those who awaken from its darkness.

————◆————

Life is the chance God gives you to develop the strength to look for and find the truth inside you.

————◆————

To save a lie is to give away the truth.

————◆————

What you are born into is what you will become and that from which you must escape if you are to find God.

————◆————

Good losers make for good winners only if they learn why they lost.

———◆———

Even the greatest of wealth cannot long afford poverty as a neighbor.

———◆———

Neither five nor five thousand followers will give a man the courage equal to a man strong enough to stand alone.

———◆———

What is beauty? Beauty is that which causes pleasure without causing harm. That is why of all things, love is most beautiful to the human soul.

———◆———

Fame does not so much remove the hungry emptiness within the soul as it does expose it and fill it with all manner of things.

———◆———

To arrive at the truth, you first must leave ignorance and then travel through dreams, fantasy, and often hell itself.

———◆———

Those who seek power first end up powerless before God. Those who seek God first enjoy the endless power of God.

———◆———

The truth is much like the wind. It can't be seen, only felt. At times, it is gentle and comforting and helpful. At other times, it moves great oceans into fury and wears down the tallest of mountains. And like the wind, truth simply is a power unto itself. We need to pay heed to that power for there is not a dream or a scheme that will change its course or protect us from its power.

———— ◆ ————

Man will always be at war with nature for he knows nature has no favorites. Like the stones rolling downhill, nature obeys laws that do not care about what gets in their way.

———— ◆ ————

More could be done with this life if we loved God more in this life.

———— ◆ ————

The nation that loses control of its children loses control of its future. The nation that does not provide for the true needs of its children does not provide for its future.

———— ◆ ————

The purpose of this life is to reach the next one just as the purpose of the seed is not to remain a seed, but to become the flower that bears the new seed.

———— ◆ ————

Remember this: heaven would be empty if it required perfection.

It is not difficult to secure peace if it's peace that you truly want. But if it's power you want, then peace is impossible.

What has more value? A profitable lie, or an unprofitable truth?

God does not shout into the ear. He whispers quietly to the inner soul. That is why He is heard only by those who want to listen.

This is not the life in which you will achieve the perfection of which you dream. This is the life in which you will suffer for the lack of it and learn to value and seek the promise of its coming.

A heavy heart makes a heavy stone even heavier. A light heart lessens any burden.

Those who are without God shall grow old, but not up.

To turn your back on what is wrong but not the wrongdoer strengthens the soul, but to turn away from what is right and those who follow the righteous path shrivels the soul. There is no room for happiness in a shriveled soul.

———◆———

It is not a wise rabbit that mocks and teases the lion. And so it is with man and God,

———◆———

Those who lead children astray are never found by God.

———◆———

Hell is the briefest, but the most agonizing moment given to some who realize that they will not live for an eternity in God's love, but rather will, in the next moment, perish for an eternity whose promise was as much theirs as anyone's.

———◆———

If you do not seek God in this life, you shall not find Him in the next.

———◆———

Where you lead children is where you will go.

———◆———

One of the heaviest burdens a man will ever carry is laziness.

When you befriend a stranger, you befriend God.

———◆———

When you give advice, good or bad, God listens, as well.

———◆———

Be where you are with God.

———◆———

If you choose not to make God a part of your life, you make the choice for Him, as well.

———◆———

You may not choose what is going to happen in life nor can you change it. You may only choose or change which side you will be on when something does happen.

———◆———

The body God has given you is the shelter of your soul, but when you truly let God live there with you, the shelter ceases to be a simple hut and becomes, instead, a mighty temple.

———◆———

Pity those who cause you harm and pain for they are without God and in for greater pain.

———— ◆ ————

The problem with the war on those things that are evil is that society builds too many fences and takes too many prisoners. One must eliminate a cancer, not isolate it, if one is to be truly free of it. Only a fool or a coward lets the wolf walk amongst the lambs and believes it will not kill again. For those who would say it is only natural for the wolf to kill the lamb for food, they themselves must then accept it is only natural for the shepherd to kill the wolf to protect his food, as well. For in choosing to kill the lambs, it is the wolf that forces man to live by his rules. Consequently, until the wolf learns otherwise, he must accept that if he chooses to kill the shepherd's lambs, then the shepherd must do what must be done. This is the meaning of "to live by the sword is to die by the sword."

———— ◆ ————

What good are concrete palaces when children are left alone to live in the moral poverty of these concrete vacuums? If we have let ourselves reach a point where both the mother and the father must leave the home to earn a basic living, when will we also then accept the children leaving the home to help? Does no one see in which direction the rock is falling?

———— ◆ ————

The seed denied what it needs to grow will never reach its full potential. And so it is with children.

———— ◆ ————

You do not need money to love God or to smile at your fellow man.

If there is any valid measure of how close a faith comes to God's truth, it is in its tolerance and respect for other faiths.

The faith that is closest to God is the faith that is last to pick up the sword.

If it is not good for your soul, it is not good for your body.

Happiness that does not come from goodness is not good happiness and will not last.

What you let into your cup is what you must drink. Choose wisely for the man too hungry for success will swallow almost anything.

The hardest thing a man will ever do in life is be good.

When you focus on yourself, you can't see God. When you examine yourself, you will see God.

Do not move so quickly through life that you miss seeing the purpose God has laid out for you.

———◆———

To believe that this life is all there is, is to believe there is no other side to the mountain.

———◆———

When it comes to caring for the spirit of the child, it has already been said that if you step on the sapling, do not expect the tree to grow straight no matter how rich the soil.

———◆———

The word "truth" is not real. Truth is a force. Just as the word "wind" cannot fill the unfurled sail, the "truth" will not move you until you unfold your soul and let its force move you in the direction of God.

———◆———

The man who lives only up to man's expectations always falls short of God's.

———◆———

To believe in man is to be a fool before God. To believe in God is to be a fool before man.

———◆———

Most men do not listen to what God wants anymore than children remain at peace in the absence of their parents.

———◦———

It is only the ignorance of our childhood that makes the adult appear so wise.

———◦———

The free market system provides for the needs of only those who have the money to shop.

———◦———

If life should teach you nothing else, it should teach you that man is ultimately disappointing and that God is ultimately fulfilling. Once this point is learned, the fool and the wise go their separate ways.

———◦———

Good intentions are like seeds sitting on a shelf. Only when they are planted can God eventually judge the quality of the harvest.

———◦———

To believe in God is to not only speak of Him, but to do His will, as well, for the true belief must be spoken and lived or it cannot be heard and seen.

———◦———

God can do no less than the best of that of which good men's souls' dream.

———◆———

Man should be married to God before being married to the flesh or the marriage to the flesh will not have a lasting spirit.

———◆———

If there is a man or nation or faith that will not see these truths, then they will not be seen by God.

———◆———

You need to take moments each day and sit quiet, still, and alone. Then you need to listen and see yourself and ask who you are without God and who you are if you are with God. To be with God is who you are. To be without God is to be no one.

———◆———

Your soul will eventually starve to death if you do not take the time to find and pick the fruit of truth and then carefully plant its seeds in new gardens.

———◆———

The emptiness you feel within yourself cannot be filled by anything in this world of man. It can only be filled by you choosing God and doing God's will.

———◆———

When you are released from your body, God does not ask of you what religion you are, but rather how much you have longed for Him and the Spirit of the Living Truth. Your answer to that and that alone determines how much of you shall be saved to live with Him for the wickedness and ignorance in you is cut away and left at the gates of death.

————◆————

Do not disrespect or disregard life in any form for all life is of God. All life.

————◆————

For each to have a turn to live without God in this life, each must have a turn to die to return to God in the next.

————◆————

Death should be feared only by the truly wicked. And who are the truly wicked? Those who deny God and worship and serve themselves over all other things. They are dead seeds that will not grow in the new garden.

————◆————

If any faith or religion separates man, it is separated from God.

————◆————

Christ did not come to change the world. He came so that you might have a chance to change.

————◆————

Be prepared and willing, for there is yet another more wondrous life coming.

———— ◆ ————

When it comes to caring for the spirit of the child, it has already been said that if you keep stepping on the sapling, do not expect it to grow straight no matter how rich the soil.

———— ◆ ————

Like the young chick, we are born in a shell of darkness and must struggle and break out if we are ever to discover the light and unfurl our wings.

———— ◆ ————

If it is to grow straight and reach its potential, the young tree must be supported and protected from the full force of the wind as surely as the youth of man must be supported and protected from the full force of a life of unrestricted freedom.

———— ◆ ————

If you would understand the application of and relative value of truth and knowledge in life, consider the man who understands the truth that an attacking tiger will kill him, but lacks the knowledge of how to defend himself. Truth is to knowledge as the bow is to the arrow. Both are needed if one is to be successful in dealing with life's tigers.

———— ◆ ————

Maturity is like a scab that protects youthful sores that require a lifetime of healing.

———— ◆ ————

Your body is no more a part of your soul than the cup is a part of the water.

———— ◆ ————

You must risk something to do something, but to do nothing is to risk everything.

———— ◆ ————

In life, truth is like a tool. It is worthless until you pick it up and learn how to use it.

———— ◆ ————

The unknowing man believes power is important as it makes him important. The knowing man knows that God is important and that gives him power.

———— ◆ ————

Until you love God, you will love neither man nor yourself. Until you serve man, you will serve neither God nor yourself.

———— ◆ ————

The wisest of the wise cannot convince a fool he is a fool, but eventually, life will do just that with unhappiness for it is the master teacher.

It is the wolf and not the shepherd that decides if the shepherd must carry a gun.

———◆———

Sad will be the children who do not give up childhood for they will be like seeds left unplanted and denied their destiny.

———◆———

You can neither see nor appreciate the true value of life until you see and accept the value of a true God.

———◆———

Men accept a faith that they might be accepted by man. But for the men who truly accept God, there is no faith, only love.

———◆———

It is impossible to be happy with who you are if you try to be what others want you to become.

———◆———

Each of us is born into our own little private frying pan and the life that follows is spent trying to find the knob that controls the temperature.

———◆———

Truth is like a mountain in a desert. You can see it from almost any place. To see it more clearly, you must move closer to it,

but to understand and know it more, you must make the effort
to climb it.

———•———

Yellow Weeds and Dead Crickets
1964

Alone, I walk in the whisper
    Of yellowed weeds that echo
The heat of a weary summer
    Almost dead and crickets tune black bows
In unsuspecting requiem for what once was mirth
    And so richly green and bold
With strength so plentiful at birth.
    Now brittle bones, the weeds no longer bend,
But move stiffly aside, half dead
    From autumn's scarlet fever come again.
As if cruel surprise has been said,
    The Earth rages red at now being told
Of its nearing fate so close ahead
    Where few will escape death's coming hold.

Wandering in the beauty of this agony
    Where crickets are the sound of summer's last night,
And a weed is the color of the golden hill I see
    Fading with the sun from my sight,
I seem immortal to them, an envy
    To generations of crickets and weeds
That will pass on tales of me to their progeny,
    Yet to bring back this beauty from eggs and seed.

I am legend to this season, this path,

> For I was here last year, this same way
> Where in passing I saw the same quiet wrath
> Take an uncomplaining land away
> Into memory and bring forth new children.
> How strange and somehow sad are these ways
> Of God to men, yet so much more peaceful than
> man to men.

———◆———

The quality of your thinking determines the quality of your life.

———◆———

If you want to change your life for the better, you must change your thoughts for the better.

———◆———

If God wanted us to only have a blind faith, He would not have given us the desire to see and understand the truth. For He has not put the glory of the heavens and the painful wetness of our blood in front of our eyes for no purpose.

———◆———

The most brilliant of jewels will not shine when there is no light anymore than the soul of man will shine without the light of God's love.

———◆———

He is nothing but a fool who would seek to fill his mind and pockets in this life until there is no room left for God.

The single quality that separates man from the rest of the animals is his ability to choose to not act like an animal and to use this free will to accept the ways of God's will.

Like the most brilliant of jewels, the truth has many facets, but they are all a part of the same stone.

To see and know of the apple is not enough. You must eat it if it is to nourish your body. And so it is with the truth which must be consumed if it is to become a part of your soul.

The truth behind these truths is yet to come, and it must wait for the coming Son whose purpose, like the sun, is to reveal the secrets hidden in this life's darkness.

The infant has no desire to leave the womb and it is only the painful effort of the mother's flesh that separates them as separate they must become if the child is to truly live. And so it is with the soul of man who has no desire to leave his womb of flesh. It takes a great deal of pain to separate the body from the sou! but that is what also must be done if the man is to truly live.

---◆---

Far From Over

Although this would appear to be the end of my search, it isn't. It is simply where I am at this moment in my life and where I pause to follow my own advice to, once again, stop and listen carefully for that inner voice for I do not want to miss it when it speaks so quietly to my soul.

In this silence, and to wherever you are in this world, I now pass on to you the opportunity to join me on the empty pages which follow by writing down what truths come from your own memories or epiphanic moments of cherished insight. Do this by listening to the tears and joys of your past, to your soul, and by watching this world we live in, then let your own inner voices speak the truth to you. Do this so you may share with others the truth you see and the real truths you've been taught or have read that have helped fill the emptiness within your soul and given you a direction in the darkness of this life.

Do it to add to the light of the candles already lit. Do it to add to the grains of truth to expand the beach and to put new stars in the heavens' darkness. Let your footprints start where mine have left off. Share the truths your own hearts have come to cherish as anchors in the churning waves of these stormy times. Together, let's build an even greater truth for ourselves and each other so that we and those yet to come may see, accept, and follow more clearly and dearly our one common God whose promise is always with us. To build that greater truth, you must question everything. To see what I am sharing, look at a quote from a very famous man who said: "Be the change you wish to see in this world."

That man was Gandhi. You may say, "Wow, that's good advice," but what if the "change" is bad, such as Hitler and other demagogues brought and bring into this world? How could Gandhi's advice be made even better? More clear? How about, "Be the change _for the better for_ _everyone_ that you wish to see in this world"? Yes! Now, there is no doubt about what "change" really should mean in the heart of man and in the heart of God.

In closing, I am not going to wish or pray that God be with you for God and Jesus Christ have always been with you, which is a truth you should accept and understand by now. No, I'm going to pray that you, in your heart, mind, and soul, are with God. For only then will you see the truth of life and understand what Christ said when He spoke the words, "The truth shall set you free" (John 8:32).

Now, I hope you can see that this life, your life, is made of either the choice of others or of your own choice, but always remember that the final judgment will be made on the choices you make, not made by others. As another old saying goes, "You are the captain of your own soul."

Printed in the USA
CPSIA information can be obtained
at www.ICGtesting.com
LVHW020824040524
778993LV00019B/735

9 781662 887178